Bible History

ABCs

Bible History ABCs: God's Story from A to Z
Text copyright © 2019 Stephen J. Nichols
Illustrations copyright © 2019 Ned Bustard

Published by Crossway
1300 Crescent Street
Wheaton, Illinois 60187

Book design and illustration: Ned Bustard
First printing 2019
Printed in China
Scripture quotations are from the ESV® Bible (The Holy Bible, English Standard Version®), copyright © 2001 by Crossway, a publishing ministry of Good News Publishers. Used by permission. All rights reserved.

ISBN: 978-1-4335-6437-6

Library of Congress Cataloging-in-Publication Data
Names: Nichols, Stephen J., 1970— author. | Bustard, Ned, illustrator.
Title: Bible history ABCs : God's story from A to Z / Stephen J. Nichols.
Description: Wheaton : Crossway, 2019.
Identifiers: LCCN 2018055382 | ISBN 9781433564376 (hc)
Subjects: LCSH: Bible—Dictionaries, Juvenile. | Bible—Criticism, interpretation, etc.—Juvenile literature.
Classification: LCC BS440 .N46 2019 | DDC 220.3—dc23
LC record available at https://lccn.loc.gov/2018055382

Crossway is a publishing ministry of Good News Publishers.
RRD   28   27   26   25   24   23   22   21   20   19
15   14   13   12   11   10   9   8   7   6   5   4   3   2   1

For my family—S. J. N.

For the PreK class at The Geneva School of Manhattan—N. B.

"I like Bibles."

—Johannes G.

STEPHEN J. NICHOLS

NED BUSTARD

Bible History

ABCs

God's Story from **A to Z**

CROSSWAY®

WHEATON, ILLINOIS

A is for aardvarks, armadillos, an apple, and

ADAM

Anchors aweigh. Let's start our journey through the Bible from beginning to end, from *A* to *Z*.

In the beginning God made all things. He made alligators and asteroids, anteaters and antelopes, and also ants. Of all the creatures God made, he made only one in his image: Adam. God did not want Adam to be alone, so God made Eve. They lived in absolute Paradise and were to worship God alone. They ate avocados and all kinds of wonderful fruit. They were not allowed to eat one forbidden fruit. Alas, they disobeyed God, ate it, and lost all Paradise.

And *in Adam's fall we sinned all.*

God sent them away from the garden, east of Eden. The Bible tells us how we get home.

"In the beginning, God created the heavens and the earth."

GENESIS 1:1

"The LORD God took the man and put him in the garden of Eden to work it and keep it. And the LORD God commanded the man, saying, 'You may surely eat of every tree of the garden, but of the tree of the knowledge of good and evil you shall not eat, for in the day that you eat of it you shall surely die.'"

GENESIS 2:15–17

"So when the woman saw that the tree was good for food, and that it was a delight to the eyes, and that the tree was to be desired to make one wise, she took of its fruit and ate, and she also gave some to her husband who was with her, and he ate. Then the eyes of both were opened, and they knew that they were naked. And they sewed fig leaves together and made themselves loincloths.

And they heard the sound of the LORD God walking in the garden in the cool of the day, and the man and his wife hid themselves from the presence of the LORD God among the trees of the garden. But the LORD God called to the man and said to him, 'Where are you?' And he said, 'I heard the sound of you in the garden, and I was afraid, because I was naked, and I hid myself.' He said, 'Who told you that you were naked? Have you eaten of the tree of which I commanded you not to eat?'"

GENESIS 3:6–11

"For as in Adam all die, so also in Christ shall all be made alive."

1 CORINTHIANS 15:22

B is for bears, balloons, bulldozers, and the
TOWER *of* BABEL

"Now the whole earth had one language and the same words. And as people migrated from the east, they found a plain in the land of Shinar and settled there. And they said to one another, 'Come, let us make bricks, and burn them thoroughly.' And they had brick for stone, and bitumen for mortar. Then they said, 'Come, let us build ourselves a city and a tower with its top in the heavens, and let us make a name for ourselves, lest we be dispersed over the face of the whole earth.' And the LORD came down to see the city and the tower, which the children of man had built. And the LORD said, 'Behold, they are one people, and they have all one language, and this is only the beginning of what they will do. And nothing that they propose to do will now be impossible for them. Come, let us go down and there confuse their language, so that they may not understand one another's speech.' So the LORD dispersed them from there over the face of all the earth, and they left off building the city. Therefore its name was called Babel, because there the LORD confused the language of all the earth. And from there the LORD dispersed them over the face of all the earth."

GENESIS 11:1–9

Many, many children were born after Adam and Eve, and many behaved very badly. God even sent a flood to judge all these people, but he saved Noah and his family. He had Noah build a very big boat, and God brought Noah and all the animals—baboons, badgers, beavers, and even buzzard birds—safely through the booming storm. But after the flood, people built a big city out of bricks, burned in an oven. They even built a big tower that stretched to the sky. They were behaving badly again. But God put an end to that.

The place was called Babel, and from that time on people started speaking different languages like Bahasa and Bengali, Bulgarian, and even British English.

C is for calves, camels, candles, and

COVENANT

On a deep dark night, God came to Abraham, saying, "Know for certain . . ." (Gen. 15:13).

What was Abraham to know? That God had called him out of the land of the Chaldeans and sent him in to the land of Canaan. That God would give him many children, more children than stars in the sky. That God chose him to be his special son, and that God chose him to be the father of his chosen nation. That dark night God made a covenant with Abraham with a smoking firepot and a flaming torch.

And what did Abraham do? Abraham believed God, and it was counted to him as righteousness. When God makes a covenant, we know for certain it will come to pass.

"Now the LORD said to Abram, 'Go from your country and your kindred and your father's house to the land that I will show you. And I will make of you a great nation, and I will bless you and make your name great, so that you will be a blessing. I will bless those who bless you, and him who dishonors you I will curse, and in you all the families of the earth shall be blessed.'"

GENESIS 12:1–3

"And he brought him outside and said, 'Look toward heaven, and number the stars, if you are able to number them.' Then he said to him, 'So shall your offspring be.' And he believed the LORD, and he counted it to him as righteousness."

GENESIS 15:5–6

"For what does the Scripture say? 'Abraham believed God, and it was counted to him as righteousness.'"

ROMANS 4:3

D is for donkeys, Dalmatians, the desert, and

DREAMS

Isaac had a son named Jacob, and of Jacob's many sons he loved Joseph the most. Jacob was devoted to Joseph and gave him a coat of many colors—it dazzled and delighted Joseph. But it brought much displeasure to his brothers. And so did Joseph's dreams. At Dothan, they threw him into a deep ditch and then sold him as a slave down to Egypt. Even in Egypt, Joseph had difficulties and ended up in a dungeon. But God had destined Joseph for great things. Joseph dreamed more dreams, and soon Pharaoh himself promoted him to second-in-command over all the dominion of Egypt. Joseph even delivered his brothers from a time of famine. They devised harm for Joseph, but God delivered him.

"Now Israel loved Joseph more than any other of his sons, because he was the son of his old age. And he made him a robe of many colors. But when his brothers saw that their father loved him more than all his brothers, they hated him and could not speak peacefully to him.

"Now Joseph had a dream, and when he told it to his brothers they hated him even more. He said to them, 'Hear this dream that I have dreamed: Behold, we were binding sheaves in the field, and behold, my sheaf arose and stood upright. And behold, your sheaves gathered around it and bowed down to my sheaf.' His brothers said to him, 'Are you indeed to reign over us? Or are you indeed to rule over us?' So they hated him even more for his dreams and for his words.

"Then he dreamed another dream and told it to his brothers and said, 'Behold, I have dreamed another dream. Behold, the sun, the moon, and eleven stars were bowing down to me.' But when he told it to his father and to his brothers, his father rebuked him and said to him, 'What is this dream that you have dreamed? Shall I and your mother and your brothers indeed come to bow ourselves to the ground before you?' And his brothers were jealous of him, but his father kept the saying in mind."

GENESIS 37:3–11

E is for eagles, ears, the emperor penguin, and the
EXODUS *out of* EGYPT

"God spoke to Moses and said to him, 'I am the LORD. I appeared to Abraham, to Isaac, and to Jacob, as God Almighty, but by my name the LORD I did not make myself known to them. I also established my covenant with them to give them the land of Canaan, the land in which they lived as sojourners. Moreover, I have heard the groaning of the people of Israel whom the Egyptians hold as slaves, and I have remembered my covenant. Say therefore to the people of Israel, 'I am the LORD, and I will bring you out from under the burdens of the Egyptians, and I will deliver you from slavery to them, and I will redeem you with an outstretched arm and with great acts of judgment. I will take you to be my people, and I will be your God, and you shall know that I am the LORD your God, who has brought you out from under the burdens of the Egyptians.'"

EXODUS 6:2–7

It was a great escape! Israel had been enduring much hardship in Egypt. Their cries reached God's ears. God enlisted Moses to be the great deliverer of his people. Moses went right into Pharaoh's expansive throne room and said, "Let my people go" (Ex. 5:1). But Pharaoh would not let them exit. God sent ten plagues as a judgment on Egypt. In one of the plagues, frogs were everywhere —even on the most expensive estates. Eventually, Pharaoh let Israel go. God had Moses take the people right through the Red Sea on dry ground. Pharaoh's army followed but God called down the walls of water and destroyed the entire Egyptian army. Israel was no longer in bondage. God set them free.

F is for fish, frogs, fan, and

FAITHFUL

So many times, and in so many ways, God's people were unfaithful to him. Adam and Eve disobeyed. Abraham and Sarah disobeyed. Isaac disobeyed. Everyone in God's big family disobeyed. But God always remains faithful. He made a covenant, and he will keep it. He alone is faithful because he alone is God. He is perfect and pure, holy and true, infinite and eternal. He never sleeps even for a wink. He is all-powerful, all-knowing, all-wise, and all-good. He never faints, never falters, and he never, never fails. God is a forgiving Father, and he will forever be faithful to his Word and his promises.

"For you are a people holy to the LORD your God. The LORD your God has chosen you to be a people for his treasured possession, out of all the peoples who are on the face of the earth. It was not because you were more in number than any other people that the LORD set his love on you and chose you, for you were the fewest of all peoples, but it is because the LORD loves you and is keeping the oath that he swore to your fathers, that the LORD has brought you out with a mighty hand and redeemed you from the house of slavery, from the hand of Pharaoh king of Egypt. Know therefore that the LORD your God is God, the faithful God who keeps covenant and steadfast love with those who love him and keep his commandments, to a thousand generations."
DEUTERONOMY 7:6–9

"The steadfast love of the
    LORD never ceases;
  his mercies never come
    to an end;
they are new every morning;
  great is your faithfulness."
    LAMENTATIONS 3:22–23

G is for geckos, giants, gophers, and
GOATS

"But when Christ appeared as a high priest of the good things that have come, then through the greater and more perfect tent (not made with hands, that is, not of this creation) he entered once for all into the holy places, not by means of the blood of goats and calves but by means of his own blood, thus securing an eternal redemption. For if the blood of goats and bulls, and the sprinkling of defiled persons with the ashes of a heifer, sanctify for the purification of the flesh, how much more will the blood of Christ, who through the eternal Spirit offered himself without blemish to God, purify our conscience from dead works to serve the living God."

HEBREWS 9:11–14

God gave Israel a great gift: *himself.* He wanted Israel as his chosen people, his prized possession. He gave them instructions on how to build a tabernacle, a giant tent made of colorful threads and gold, gold, gold everywhere. God wanted to dwell with his people. But he is holy, and we are not. We are guilty. So God also gave Israel instructions for sacrifices. All of these sacrifices pointed to the gift of God's own Son.

Jesus would be the ultimate sacrifice for our sins, remove our guilt, and gain our salvation. Without the shedding of blood, there is no forgiveness of sins. Israel was grateful for goats and lambs. And we are grateful for the gift of the spotless Lamb.

H is for hamsters, horns, hammerhead sharks, and
HELMETS

"Sound the horns. Hurry! Hold up your shields and hoist up your swords."

Joshua's mighty warriors heard these words many times. They put on their helmets and marched off to war. The Hebrews were conquering the Holy Land. But in one of the most famous battles they didn't need helmets, shields, or swords. They marched around the city and hollered and blew on rams' horns. And on the seventh day, after the seventh time, guess what happened? The walls of Jericho came tumbling down. How's that?

We have many heroes in helmets, but this story reminds us that God is the Hero of his story.

Hallelujah.

"Now Jericho was shut up inside and outside because of the people of Israel. None went out, and none came in. And the LORD said to Joshua, 'See, I have given Jericho into your hand, with its king and mighty men of valor. You shall march around the city, all the men of war going around the city once. Thus shall you do for six days. Seven priests shall bear seven trumpets of rams' horns before the ark. On the seventh day you shall march around the city seven times, and the priests shall blow the trumpets. And when they make a long blast with the ram's horn, when you hear the sound of the trumpet, then all the people shall shout with a great shout, and the wall of the city will fall down flat, and the people shall go up, everyone straight before him.' . . .

"On the seventh day they rose early, at the dawn of day, and marched around the city in the same manner seven times. It was only on that day that they marched around the city seven times. And at the seventh time, when the priests had blown the trumpets, Joshua said to the people, 'Shout, for the LORD has given you the city.' . . . So the people shouted, and the trumpets were blown. As soon as the people heard the sound of the trumpet, the people shouted a great shout, and the wall fell down flat, so that the people went up into the city, every man straight before him, and they captured the city. Then they devoted all in the city to destruction, both men and women, young and old, oxen, sheep, and donkeys, with the edge of the sword."

JOSHUA 6:1–5, 15–16, 20–21

I is for insects, indigo, Indian elephants, and

IDOLS

Why did God insist that Joshua and his mighty warriors drive out all the inhabitants of the land of Canaan? Because they had idols. There were idols everywhere. Idols in Jericho, idols in Ai, and idols in Philistia. Back in Egypt they had thousands of idols. In those days people made idols out of wood, stone, silver, and gold. They painted their idols indigo. They made idols of animals and even of insects.

God wanted to keep his people from all these idols. He wanted Israel to worship him alone. Idols can't see. Idols don't hear. Idols will even topple over. But God sees and hears, and he never totters or wobbles. He is the living and true God indeed.

"You shall not make idols for yourselves or erect an image or pillar, and you shall not set up a figured stone in your land to bow down to it, for I am the LORD your God."

LEVITICUS 26:1

"And we know that the Son of God has come and has given us understanding, so that we may know him who is true; and we are in him who is true, in his Son Jesus Christ. He is the true God and eternal life. Little children, keep yourselves from idols."

I JOHN 5:20–21

J is for jellyfish, the jungle, jack-o-lanterns, and

JUDGES

"And the people of Israel did what was evil in the sight of the LORD and served the Baals. And they abandoned the LORD, the God of their fathers, who had brought them out of the land of Egypt. They went after other gods, from among the gods of the peoples who were around them, and bowed down to them. And they provoked the LORD to anger."

JUDGES 2:11–12

"And what more shall I say? For time would fail me to tell of Gideon, Barak, Samson, Jephthah, of David and Samuel and the prophets—who through faith conquered kingdoms, enforced justice, obtained promises, stopped the mouths of lions, quenched the power of fire, escaped the edge of the sword, were made strong out of weakness, became mighty in war, put foreign armies to flight."

HEBREWS 11:32–34

Judges wear robes, jump up to the bench, and judge all things. Right? In the Bible, judges also deliver God's people. Israel would forget God and foolishly follow after idols. They would cry out to be delivered, and God would send a judge. It was a time of sin and judgment because God is just. It was also a time of salvation and deliverance because God is merciful. God sent judges like Gideon, Deborah, and Jephthah.

God also sent a judge named Samson. He took honey from a swarm of bees, and he once used the jawbone of a donkey to strike down one thousand men. But Samson was not perfect. He too sinned. Even judges needed a deliverer. And someday that Judge would come.

K is for kangaroo, kingfisher, king crabs, and David the

KING

Israel chose Saul to be their first king. But Saul soon stopped following God, and Saul could no longer be king of God's kingdom. God then chose David, a shepherd, to be king. David knew he could put his trust in God. He killed bears and lions when they attacked his sheep. And when Goliath kicked dirt in the face of the whole army of Israel, David alone stood up and knocked the big giant down.

David was a mighty king and he was a keen musician. But he didn't always keep God's commands. Many kings followed David. Only a few were kind and good, most were bad.

God's people kept waiting and waiting for the perfect King to come.

"So David prevailed over [Goliath] with a sling and with a stone, and struck the Philistine and killed him. There was no sword in the hand of David. Then David ran and stood over the Philistine and took his sword and drew it out of its sheath and killed him and cut off his head with it. When the Philistines saw that their champion was dead, they fled. And the men of Israel and Judah rose with a shout and pursued the Philistines as far as Gath and the gates of Ekron, so that the wounded Philistines fell on the way from Shaaraim as far as Gath and Ekron. And the people of Israel came back from chasing the Philistines, and they plundered their camp. And David took the head of the Philistine and brought it to Jerusalem, but he put his armor in his tent. . . .

"As they were coming home, when David returned from striking down the Philistine, the women came out of all the cities of Israel, singing and dancing, to meet King Saul, with tambourines, with songs of joy, and with musical instruments. And the women sang to one another as they celebrated,

'Saul has struck down his thousands,
and David his ten thousands.'"

I SAMUEL 17:50–54; 18:6–7

L is for lambs, leopards, lyrics, and
LYRE

A lyre is not a liar. A lyre is an old-time musical instrument with strings. It was shaped like a *U*, not an *L*. The Bible is full of musical instruments like horns and harps, pipes played by pipers, and lyres and lutes.

The famous preacher Martin Luther played a lute, but King David liked to strum a tune on a lyre. David wrote many psalms—including Psalm 33. The streets were lined with musicians, and choirs would loudly sing the psalms. They sang of lads and lasses who loved God. They lifted God's name high.

The people loved to listen because they needed to hear about God and learn all that he had done and all that he would do. They sang praises to the Lord throughout all the land.

"Shout for joy in the LORD, O you righteous!
    Praise befits the upright.
Give thanks to the LORD with the lyre;
    make melody to him with the harp of ten strings!
Sing to him a new song;
    play skillfully on the strings, with loud shouts.
For the word of the LORD is upright,
    and all his work is done in faithfulness.
He loves righteousness and justice;
    the earth is full of the steadfast love of the LORD."

PSALM 33:1–5

M is for magpies, mules, matches, and the last prophet—
MALACHI

"For behold, the day is coming, burning like an oven, when all the arrogant and all evildoers will be stubble. The day that is coming shall set them ablaze, says the LORD of hosts, so that it will leave them neither root nor branch. But for you who fear my name, the sun of righteousness shall rise with healing in its wings. You shall go out leaping like calves from the stall. And you shall tread down the wicked, for they will be ashes under the soles of your feet, on the day when I act, says the LORD of hosts."

MALACHI
4:1–3

God sent his messenger Malachi to the people of Israel. Malachi said a servant honors his master, but Israel no longer honored God. Israel needed to remember that God is the mighty King. He matters the most. God loved his people, and he said, "They shall be mine and make up my treasured possession."

Malachi prophesied of another messenger to come, a forerunner who would make a path for the perfect Judge, the perfect Prophet, the perfect Priest, and the perfect King to come. And make no mistake about it, when God makes a promise, he will always keep it—not some of the time, not most of the time, but all of the time.

N is for narwhals, nightingales, nets, and NAZARETH

Follow a straight line on a map up from the city of Jerusalem and you come to the little town of Nazareth. Jesus was born in Bethlehem, but he grew up in Nazareth. Nazareth is also where the angel Gabriel appeared to the virgin Mary and announced that she would have a son named Jesus. Mary said, "My soul magnifies the Lord . . . holy is his name" (Luke 1:46, 49). Jesus, truly God, became flesh, truly man.

Jesus was a normal boy, but he never, no never, not even once, sinned. When he was all grown up, he went into the synagogue at Nazareth and read from the scroll of Isaiah and said, "Today this Scripture has been fulfilled" (Luke 4:21).

In Nazareth, the King had come.

"In the sixth month the angel Gabriel was sent from God to a city of Galilee named Nazareth, to a virgin betrothed to a man whose name was Joseph, of the house of David. And the virgin's name was Mary. And he came to her and said, 'Greetings, O favored one, the Lord is with you!' But she was greatly troubled at the saying, and tried to discern what sort of greeting this might be. And the angel said to her, 'Do not be afraid, Mary, for you have found favor with God. And behold, you will conceive in your womb and bear a son, and you shall call his name Jesus. He will be great and will be called the Son of the Most High. And the Lord God will give to him the throne of his father David, and he will reign over the house of Jacob forever, and of his kingdom there will be no end.'"

LUKE 1:26–33

O is for otters, oranges, octopuses, and the
MOUNT *of* OLIVES

"As the mountains surround Jerusalem,
    so the LORD surrounds his people,
    from this time forth and forevermore."

PSALM 125:2

"Now when all the people were baptized, and when Jesus also had been baptized and was praying, the heavens were opened, and the Holy Spirit descended on him in bodily form, like a dove; and a voice came from heaven, 'You are my beloved Son; with you I am well pleased.' . . .

    "And Jesus, full of the Holy Spirit, returned from the Jordan and was led by the Spirit in the wilderness for forty days, being tempted by the devil. And he ate nothing during those days. And when they were ended, he was hungry."

LUKE 3:21–22; 4:1–2

"And he came out and went, as was his custom, to the Mount of Olives, and the disciples followed him."

LUKE 22:39

"And when they had sung a hymn, they went out to the Mount of Olives."

MATTHEW 26:30

An octopus lives down in the sea, an owl lives up in a tree, and Jesus lived on earth like you and me. He went to ordinary places and did ordinary things that all ordinary boys do. Then one day John baptized Jesus in the Jordan River. From then on Jesus taught big crowds in the open air and performed miracles like opening blind eyes.

Jesus still went to ordinary places. He often went to the Mount of Olives. It overlooked old Jerusalem and overflowed with ancient and gnarled olive trees. Here Jesus once prayed all night to obey God's will. Of all the ordinary things Jesus did, one was not. He was perfectly obedient, not only often, but all of the time.

P is for perch, pike, puffer fish, and one of the twelve disciples—

PETER

Peter had been fishing all night and had caught nothing. Period. Then Jesus popped into his boat, and they pushed out to sea. Jesus said, "Let down your nets" (Luke 5:4). When they pulled in the nets, they had a great big pile of fish. Then Jesus said to Peter, "Follow me" (Matt. 4:19). Peter promptly put down his nets and followed him.

Jesus picked Peter, and he picked eleven others to be the twelve disciples. They followed him everywhere, even on paths through the prairie. Some nights they slept under the stars and planets and had rocks for pillows. Peter penned two epistles. In them Peter praised God for pardoning all his sins through the precious blood of his Master, Jesus.

"Getting into one of the boats, which was Simon's, [Jesus] asked him to put out a little from the land. And he sat down and taught the people from the boat.

"And when he had finished speaking, he said to Simon, 'Put out into the deep and let down your nets for a catch.' And Simon answered, 'Master, we toiled all night and took nothing! But at your word I will let down the nets.' And when they had done this, they enclosed a large number of fish, and their nets were breaking. They signaled to their partners in the other boat to come and help them. And they came and filled both the boats, so that they began to sink. But when Simon Peter saw it, he fell down at Jesus' knees, saying, 'Depart from me, for I am a sinful man, O Lord.' For he and all who were with him were astonished at the catch of fish that they had taken, and so also were James and John, sons of Zebedee, who were partners with Simon. And Jesus said to Simon, 'Do not be afraid; from now on you will be catching men.' And when they had brought their boats to land, they left everything and followed him."

LUKE 5:3–11

Q is for queen angelfish, quiver, quilt, and
QUESTIONS

"This is why I speak to them in parables, because seeing they do not see, and hearing they do not hear, nor do they understand. Indeed, in their case the prophecy of Isaiah is fulfilled that says:

'"You will indeed hear but never understand, and you will indeed see but never perceive." For this people's heart has grown dull, and with their ears they can barely hear, and their eyes they have closed, lest they should see with their eyes and hear with their ears and understand with their heart and turn, and I would heal them.'

But blessed are your eyes, for they see, and your ears, for they hear."

MATTHEW
13:13–16

QUESTION: *How did Jesus teach?*
ANSWER: *By asking questions.*

Jesus spent three years teaching, performing miracles, and training his twelve disciples. He quested all around Israel. Sometimes he traveled quickly, sometimes quietly. But he always loved to teach people about God.

He had a big quantity of quotations from the Old Testament that he would quote a lot. He also taught in parables. And he loved to teach by asking questions. He asked the Pharisees questions, and they quarreled. One time he asked his disciples a very important question: "Who do you say that I am?" Peter quickly answered as clearly as quartz crystal: "You are the Christ, the Son of the living God" (Matt. 16:15–16).

R is for raccoons, roosters, rivers, and
RESURRECTION

"But on the first day of the week, at early dawn, they went to the tomb, taking the spices they had prepared. And they found the stone rolled away from the tomb, but when they went in they did not find the body of the Lord Jesus. While they were perplexed about this, behold, two men stood by them in dazzling apparel. And as they were frightened and bowed their faces to the ground, the men said to them, 'Why do you seek the living among the dead? He is not here, but has risen. Remember how he told you, while he was still in Galilee, that the Son of Man must be delivered into the hands of sinful men and be crucified and on the third day rise.' And they remembered his words, and returning from the tomb they told all these things to the eleven and to all the rest. Now it was Mary Magdalene and Joanna and Mary the mother of James and the other women with them who told these things to the apostles, but these words seemed to them an idle tale, and they did not believe them. But Peter rose and ran to the tomb; stooping and looking in, he saw the linen cloths by themselves; and he went home marveling at what had happened."

LUKE 24:1–12

The religious teachers rejected Jesus and replied: "You are not our King." They plotted to have Jesus arrested, and raised a rabble crowd. Jesus was beaten and given a crown of thorns and a hard, rough robe to mock him. He was ordered to carry his own cross. Roman soldiers raised the cross, and there Jesus died. He was buried, and Roman soldiers rolled a big rock in front of the tomb. But that rock was powerless.

On the third day, God raised Jesus from the dead. The disciples ran to the tomb, but Jesus was not there. He was risen. Jesus really lived. He really died. He really rose again. And all those who rest their faith in Christ will someday rise again.

S is for snails, sparrows, scrolls, and SALVATION

After Jesus returned to his throne in heaven, his disciples shared the good news of salvation to all people on every spot on the earth. Peter started first. He stood up and said:

"God will pour out [his] Spirit. . . . And it shall come to pass that everyone who calls upon the name of the Lord shall be saved" (Acts 2:17, 21).

Even before the first sunrise ever, God planned to save his people. He knew they would sin, and he knew they needed a Savior.

Jesus is the true Prophet, who speaks true sayings. He's the true Priest, who suffered and made the perfect sacrifice for sin. He's the true King, who reigns supreme. He's the only sufficient Savior. Go shout the good news.

"'And it shall come to pass that everyone who calls upon the name of the Lord shall be saved.'
"Men of Israel, hear these words: Jesus of Nazareth, a man attested to you by God with mighty works and wonders and signs that God did through him in your midst, as you yourselves know—this Jesus, delivered up according to the definite plan and foreknowledge of God, you crucified and killed by the hands of lawless men. God raised him up, loosing the pangs of death, because it was not possible for him to be held by it."

ACTS 2:21–24

"For all have sinned and fall short of the glory of God, and are justified by his grace as a gift, through the redemption that is in Christ Jesus."

ROMANS 3:23–24

"How shall we escape if we neglect such a great salvation? It was declared at first by the Lord, and it was attested to us by those who heard."

HEBREWS 2:3

T is for tummies, tigers, toads, and
TIMOTHY

"But as for you, continue in what you have learned and have firmly believed, knowing from whom you learned it and how from childhood you have been acquainted with the sacred writings, which are able to make you wise for salvation through faith in Christ Jesus. All Scripture is breathed out by God and profitable for teaching, for reproof, for correction, and for training in righteousness, that the man of God may be complete, equipped for every good work."

2 TIMOTHY 3:14–17

From the time Timothy was a toddler, his family taught him to hold on as tight as a tiger to the Christian faith. Later, Timothy had a very special teacher, the apostle Paul.

Take a look at the New Testament. Paul wrote thirteen of the twenty-seven books. He wrote to the Thessalonians and to the believers in Rome. He wrote a letter to Titus. And he wrote two letters to Timothy. When people looked down on Timothy because he was young, Paul told Timothy to stand tall during those trials and keep testifying to the truth. Paul taught Timothy to be a good soldier.

One of the very last things Paul said to Timothy was: "To the King . . . the only God, be honor and glory forever and ever. Amen" (1 Tim. 1:17).

U is for urchins in the sea, umbrella, unicorn, and
UNFADING

Pretty much everything we know fades. The energy of puppies fades. They have so much energy—until they grow up. Then they would rather unwind on the couch. Sea urchins line the ocean floor in rainbows of color, but soon they fade. Ultra Red flowers fade. Green leaves turn brilliant colors under fall skies. Then they turn brown, unhook from tree branches, and fall to the ground. But the Bible says there is something that is unfading. U have an inheritance in heaven, and that inheritance is our salvation in Jesus.

Our salvation is imperishable. It never goes yucky or stale. It is undefiled. It is always clean and pure and unusually white. And it is unfading. It will never, never fade away.

"Blessed be the God and Father of our Lord Jesus Christ! According to his great mercy, he has caused us to be born again to a living hope through the resurrection of Jesus Christ from the dead, to an inheritance that is imperishable, undefiled, and unfading, kept in heaven for you, who by God's power are being guarded through faith for a salvation ready to be revealed in the last time. In this you rejoice, though now for a little while, if necessary, you have been grieved by various trials, so that the tested genuineness of your faith—more precious than gold that perishes though it is tested by fire—may be found to result in praise and glory and honor at the revelation of Jesus Christ. Though you have not seen him, you love him. Though you do not now see him, you believe in him and rejoice with joy that is inexpressible and filled with glory, obtaining the outcome of your faith, the salvation of your souls."

1 PETER 1:3–9

V is for victory, vase, violet, and
VINE

"I am the true vine, and my Father is the vinedresser. Every branch in me that does not bear fruit he takes away, and every branch that does bear fruit he prunes, that it may bear more fruit. Already you are clean because of the word that I have spoken to you. Abide in me, and I in you. As the branch cannot bear fruit by itself, unless it abides in the vine, neither can you, unless you abide in me. I am the vine; you are the branches. Whoever abides in me and I in him, he it is that bears much fruit, for apart from me you can do nothing."

JOHN 15:1–5

"For you were called to freedom, brothers. Only do not use your freedom as an opportunity for the flesh, but through love serve one another. For the whole law is fulfilled in one word: 'You shall love your neighbor as yourself.'. . . But the fruit of the Spirit is love, joy, peace, patience, kindness, goodness, faithfulness gentleness, self-control; against such things there is no law. And those who belong to Christ Jesus have crucified the flesh with its passions and desires. If we live by the Spirit, let us also keep in step with the Spirit."

GALATIANS 5:13–14, 22–25

Jesus told his disciples that he was many things: a Good Shepherd, a Spotless Lamb, a Door, and the Light of the World. He also said he is the true Vine, and we are the branches. Vines and vineyards were all over the valleys of Israel. Grapes grow on vines. Tomatoes, strawberries, and even kiwi grow on vines. Big juicy watermelons grow on vines. So do Christians. When we stick very close to the Vine, we grow.

Paul once said we should bear the fruit of the Spirit. When we are connected to the Vine, we grow love, joy, peace, patience, kindness, goodness, faithfulness, gentleness, and self-control. How can we be valiant, victorious, and never be vanquished? Verily, verily, stay very close to the Vine.

W is for woodpeckers, whales, walruses, and

WORSHIP

What is worship? We all worship something. People who worshiped idols were often worshiping animals. That doesn't work well at all. Animals don't want to be worshiped. They actually want to worship God. Woodpeckers worship God when they sing in the woodlands. Whales worship God when they wail in the waves. And a walrus worships God when it wobbles as it walks.

When we look into heaven in John's book of Revelation, what do we see? We see angels with wings, and fantastic creatures. And we see whole big choirs. And they all are worshiping God, singing: "Worthy is the Lamb who was slain" (Rev. 5:12). We were made to worship. We will worship God forever, and the worship chorus goes like this . . .

"And they sang a new song, saying,

"'Worthy are you to take the scroll and to open its seals, for you were slain, and by your blood you ransomed people for God from every tribe and language and people and nation, and you have made them a kingdom and priests to our God, and they shall reign on the earth.'

"Then I looked, and I heard around the throne and the living creatures and the elders the voice of many angels, numbering myriads of myriads and thousands of thousands, saying with a loud voice,

"'Worthy is the Lamb who was slain, to receive power and wealth and wisdom and might and honor and glory and blessing!'

"And I heard every creature in heaven and on earth and under the earth and in the sea, and all that is in them, saying,

"'To him who sits on the throne and to the Lamb be blessing and honor and glory and might forever and ever!'

"And the four living creatures said, 'Amen!' and the elders fell down and worshiped."

REVELATION
5:9–14

X is for . . .

X

When pirates hid their treasure, they marked the exact spot on the map with a big *X*.

The Bible is one big treasure map that points to one spot. The Old Testament pointed to this very spot. All of the New Testament points to this very spot, too. That spot, marked with an *X*, is Christ.

The first letter of Christ's name in English is the letter *C*. In Greek his first letter is *X*. The letter *X* is also in *ixthus*—the Greek word for fish. Early Christians used the symbol of the fish as their secret sign. Each letter represents a word: **I**: Jesus, **X**: Christ, **TH**: God, **U**: Son, **S**: Savior—*Jesus Christ is God's Son, our Savior. X marks the spot!*

"Long ago, at many times and in many ways, God spoke to our fathers by the prophets, but in these last days he has spoken to us by his Son, whom he appointed the heir of all things, through whom also he created the world. He is the radiance of the glory of God and the exact imprint of his nature, and he upholds the universe by the word of his power. After making purification for sins, he sat down at the right hand of the Majesty on high, having become as much superior to angels as the name he has inherited is more excellent than theirs."

HEBREWS 1:1–4

Y is for the yellow baboon, the yellow mongoose, just plain yellow, and

YEARS

"But do not overlook this one fact, beloved, that with the Lord one day is as a thousand years, and a thousand years as one day. The Lord is not slow to fulfill his promise as some count slowness, but is patient toward you, not wishing that any should perish, but that all should reach repentance. But the day of the Lord will come like a thief, and then the heavens will pass away with a roar, and the heavenly bodies will be burned up and dissolved, and the earth and the works that are done on it will be exposed.

"Since all these things are thus to be dissolved, what sort of people ought you to be in lives of holiness and godliness, waiting for and hastening the coming of the day of God, because of which the heavens will be set on fire and dissolved, and the heavenly bodies will melt as they burn! But according to his promise we are waiting for new heavens and a new earth in which righteousness dwells.

"Therefore, beloved, since you are waiting for these, be diligent to be found by him without spot or blemish, and at peace."

2 PETER
3:8–14

The yellow baboon lives to be forty-five years old. That's long, but not nearly as long as one thousand years. The Bible says that with the Lord one day is like a thousand years. That's long.

When God promised Adam and Eve a son to deliver them, it took many, many years before Jesus came. Before Jesus went up, up, up into the sky, he told his disciples that he would come back. That was many, many years ago. We wait and we wait. Peter said, "Since you are waiting for these, be diligent" (2 Pet. 3:14). God knows the perfect time for everything. He wants you to use the years of your life to serve him and tell as many people as you can about Jesus your Savior.

Z is for zebra, zeal, zipper, and ZION

"Great is the LORD and greatly to be praised
    in the city of our God!
His holy mountain, beautiful in elevation,
    is the joy of all the earth,
Mount Zion, in the far north,
    the city of the great King.
Within her citadels God
    has made himself known as a fortress. . . .
We have thought on your steadfast love, O God,
    in the midst of your temple.
As your name, O God,
    so your praise reaches to the ends of the earth.
Your right hand is filled with righteousness.
    Let Mount Zion be glad!
Let the daughters of Judah rejoice
    because of your judgments!
Walk about Zion, go around her,
    number her towers,
consider well her ramparts,
    go through her citadels,
that you may tell the next generation
    that this is God,
our God forever and ever.
    He will guide us forever."

PSALM 48:1–3, 9–14

From Adam to Zacchaeus, God has been bringing his people back home. With zeal the psalmist sang songs of Mount Zion on a zither. Zoom through the prophets. Zechariah said the King is coming to his holy mountain, and Zephaniah said, "Fear not, O Zion" (Zeph. 3:16). Zig and zag through the books of the New Testament, and you will find Mount Zion all over the pages, not quite a zillion times, but a lot. Zip up to the book of Hebrews, and you're in the zone: "You have come to Mount Zion and to the city of the living God" (Heb. 12:22).

But we still need to reach the zenith in the last book of the Bible, Revelation: "Then I looked, and behold, on Mount Zion stood the Lamb" (Rev. 14:1).

Everything has a **HISTORY**, even

THE BIBLE

The Bible was written over 1,500 years ago in Hebrew, Greek, and a tiny bit in Aramaic. It was written on long, long scrolls and on pieces of paper made from reeds and called papyrus. These pages were gathered together and called a *Biblion*—a book. During the Middle Ages, scribes sat at desks all day long and hand-copied pages, illuminating them with colorful art and fanciful letters. Then along came Gutenberg and his printing press. Today, parts of the Bible are available in almost three thousand languages, including English.

The writing on the **MOABITE STONE** goes all the way back to 800 BC. It mentions the nation of Israel and God's name, Yahweh.

One of the most fascinating scrolls found in the caves near the Dead Sea is the **ISAIAH SCROLL** from the second century BC.

Made from reeds, this **PAPYRUS TEXT** is of 2 Corinthians 11 and dates to AD 175.

Famous for its colorful pictures of mythical beasts and Celtic knots, the **BOOK OF KELLS** from AD 800 has all four of the Gospels— and it was all done by hand.

The first big book to come off the movable type printing press was the **GUTENBERG BIBLE**. The surviving copies are very rare and among the most valuable books in the world.

The first German **TRANSLATION** of the whole Bible was published in 1534, thanks to the work of Martin Luther. His friend Lucas Cranach provided over one hundred pictures for illustrations.

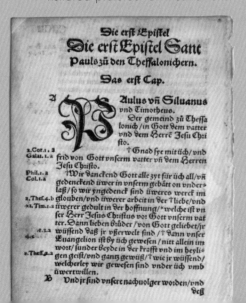

We have lots of **BIBLES TODAY** in lots of languages and in all kinds of formats, but there are still many people in the world who don't have a Bible.

Books of the **Bible**

PENTATEUCH

Genesis
Exodus
Leviticus
Numbers
Deuteronomy

HISTORY

Joshua
Judges
Ruth
1 & 2 Samuel
1 & 2 Kings
1 & 2 Chronicles
Ezra
Nehemiah
Esther

WISDOM

Job
Psalms
Proverbs
Ecclesiastes
Song of Solomon

MAJOR PROPHETS

Isaiah
Jeremiah
Lamentations
Ezekiel
Daniel

MINOR PROPHETS

Hosea
Joel
Amos
Obadiah
Jonah
Micah
Nahum
Habakkuk
Zephaniah
Haggai
Zechariah
Malachi

GOSPELS

Matthew
Mark
Luke
John
Acts

PAUL'S EPISTLES

Romans
1 & 2 Corinthians
Galatians
Ephesians
Philippians
Colossians
1 & 2 Thessalonians
1 & 2 Timothy
Titus
Philemon

GENERAL EPISTLES

Hebrews
James
1 & 2 Peter
1, 2 & 3 John
Jude

APOCALYPTIC EPISTLE

Revelation

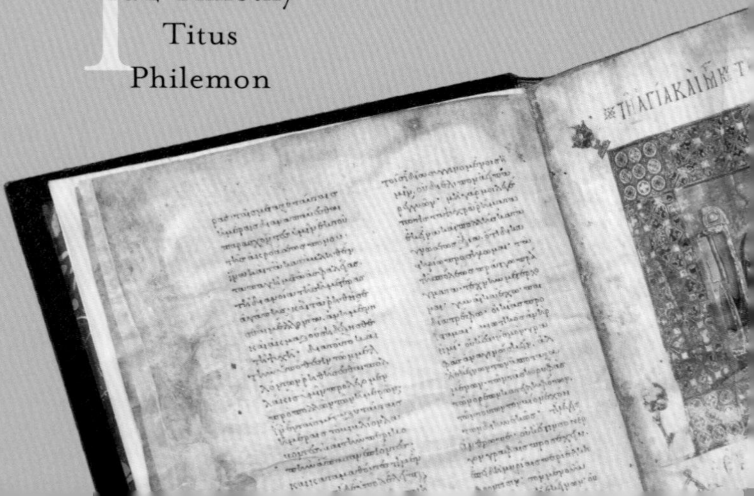

Numbers of the **Bible**

ONE Story
—God's Story

TWO Testaments

SIX Days
of Creation

TEN Commandments

SIXTY-SIX
Books

**ONE THOUSAND
ONE HUNDRED
EIGHTY-NINE**
Chapters

**THIRTY-ONE THOUSAND,
ONE HUNDRED TWO** Verses

About the ART

Most of the fine art in this book comes from the collection of The Metropolitan Museum of Art (see www.metmuseum.org/art/collection). If you visit New York City, why not take this book along? You could go on a scavenger hunt through the museum and try to find some of these works of art.*

Dedication page:
  Manuscript Leaf with the Opening of the Epistle of Saint Paul to the Ephesians, from a French Bible (ca. 1300), Met

A: *The Tree of Life* (seventeenth century), Met
B: *The (Great) Tower of Babel* (1563) by Pieter Bruegel the Elder, Kunsthistorisches Museum, Vienna, Wikimedia Commons
C: *Landscape with Stars* (ca. 1905–8) by Henri-Edmond Cross, Met
F: *Moses Shown the Promised Land* (1801) by Benjamin West, Met
G: *The Scapegoat* by William Holman Hunt, Manchester Art Gallery, Wikimedia Commons
H: *Helmets* (various time periods), Met
I: *Enthroned Canaanite deity* (Late Bronze Age), Met
K: *David* (ca. 1408–10) by Lorenzo Monaco, Met
N: *The Annunciation* (1480–89) by Hans Memling, Met
O: *Women Picking Olives* (1889) by Vincent van Gogh, Met
Q: *Golden Jubilee Medal of Queen Victoria* (1887) by Joseph Edgar Boehm, Met
R: *Pious Women at the Tomb* (1438–50) by Fra Angelico Museo di San Marco (From a scannable Dover Pictorial Archive Series book. Graphics of this kind are free to use for any purpose.)
S: *Plaque with the Pentecost* (ca. 1150–75), Met Cloisters
T: *Marble Head of a Youth* (Roman copy of work attributed to Polykleitos, ca. 41–54), Met
U: *The Unicorn in Captivity* (from the Unicorn Tapestries, ca. 1495–1505), Met Cloisters
V: *Grape Vines and Fruit, with Three Wagtails* (ca. 1615–18) by Bartolomeo Cavarozzi, Met
W: *The Adoration of the Mystic Lamb* (1432) by Jan Van Eyck, Saint Bavo Cathedral, Wikimedia Commons
X: *Faience Aryballos (oil flask) in the form of a fish* (Greek, sixth century BC), Met
Z: *The Cloisters Apocalypse* (French illuminated manuscript, ca. 1330), Met Cloisters

History:
  Book of Kells, Christ Enthroned (ninth century), Trinity College, Dublin, Wikimedia Commons
  First German translation of the Bible (1534), The Bowden Collection (used by permission)
  Gutenberg Bible (1455), The Morgan Library & Museum, Wikimedia Commons
  Isaiah Scroll (second century BC), The Israel Museum, Jerusalem, Wikimedia Commons
  Moabite Stone (800 BC), Louvre Museum, Paris, Wikimedia Commons
  Papyrus Text Commons (AD 175), Wikimedia Commons

Books:
  Jaharis Byzantine Lectionary (Byzantine illuminated manuscript, ca. 1100), Met

Numbers:
  The Creation of the World and the Expulsion from Paradise (1445) by Giovanni di Paolo, Met

*NOTE: The art on display at the Met changes periodically, so some of these pieces may not be able to be seen during your visit.

GOD'S STORY
goes on and on!

History
didn't stop at the end of the Bible. Learn more about how God's kingdom has grown through ***The Church History ABCs*** and ***Reformation ABCs.***

"The third book in this series and I *still* don't get a page!"

—Henry VIII